His Heart Calls

366-Day Devotional
HIS HEART CALLS: Love notes from God's Word
Created by Kathleen Schubitz

Copyright © 2013-2016 by Kathleen Schubitz

Published by:
RPJ & COMPANY, INC.
www.rpjandco.com | www.rpjandco1417.com
Orlando, Florida, U.S.A.

All rights reserved. No part of this devotional may be reproduced or transmitted in any form or by any means, electronic or mechanical, including photocopying, recording, or by any information storage and retrieval system, without written permission from the author or publisher, except for the inclusion of brief quotations in a review. For information, please contact the publisher.

ISBN-13: 978-1-937770-36-5

Cover and Interior Design by Kathleen Schubitz
Cover illustration: © VectorShots.com - Fotolia.com

Scriptures used herein are based on the King James Version of the Bible. Moderate word changes have been made so they appear consistent as a love letter from God, direct encouragement from Him to the reader.

Printed in the United States of America

366-Day Devotional
Love notes from God's Word

His Heart Calls

Created by
KATHLEEN SCHUBITZ

January 1

Beloved, if your heart condemn you not, then you have confidence toward Me.

1 John 3:21

January 2

But I commended My love toward you, in that, while you were yet a sinner, Christ died for you.

Romans 5:8

All scripture has been modified for personal edification and encouragement.

January 3

I have called you out of darkness into the marvelous light.

1 Peter 2:9

January 4

Cast all your care upon Me; for I careth for you.

1 Peter 5:7

All scripture has been modified for personal edification and encouragement.

January 5

*My Grace
is sufficient for you:
For My strength
is made perfect
in your weakness.*

2 Corinthians 12:9

January 6

*I, the Lord, go before thee;
I will be with thee,
I will not fail thee,
neither forsake thee:
fear not, neither
be dismayed.*

Deuteronomy 31:8

All scripture has been modified for personal edification and encouragement.

January 7

You are a new creature in Christ; old things are passed away; Behold, all things are become new.

2 Corinthians 5:17

January 8

I have blessed you with all spiritual blessings in heavenly places in Christ.

Ephesians 1:3

All scripture has been modified for personal edification and encouragement.

January 9

*You are able to do
exceeding abundantly
above all that
you ask or think,
according to the power
that worketh in you.*

Ephesians 3:20

January 10

*If you soweth
to the Spirit
ye shall reap
life everlasting.*

Galatians 6:8

All scripture has been modified for personal edification and encouragement.

January 11

Speak to yourselves in psalms and hymns and spiritual songs, singing and making melody in your heart unto Me!

Ephesians 5:19

January 12

If I am for you, who can be against you?

Romans 8:31b

All scripture has been modified for personal edification and encouragement.

January 13

You were created in My own image.

Genesis 1:27

January 14

And I will make My covenant between Me and thee, and shall multiply thee exceedingly.

Genesis 17:2

All scripture has been modified for personal edification and encouragement.

January 15

*I will
never
leave thee,
nor
forsake thee.*

Hebrews 13:5

January 16

*As you come boldly
unto the throne of grace,
you will obtain mercy,
and find grace
to help in time
of need.*

Hebrews 4:16

All scripture has been modified for personal edification and encouragement.

January 17

Fear thou not, for I am with thee... I am thy God. I will strengthen thee; I will help thee; I will uphold thee with the right hand of My righteousness.

Isaiah 41:10

January 18

Jesus was wounded for your transgressions, He was bruised for your iniquities ... and with His stripes you are healed.

Isaiah 53:5

All scripture has been modified for personal edification and encouragement.

January 19

As you delight
yourself in Me,
I will cause thee
to ride upon
the high places
of the earth...

Isaiah 58:14

January 20

Then shall My light
break forth as the morning, and
thine health shall spring
forth speedily: and thy
righteousness shall
go before thee . . .

Isaiah 58:8

All scripture has been modified for personal edification and encouragement.

January 21

*Every good gift
and every perfect gift
is from above,
and cometh down
from Me, the Father
of the children of light.*

James 1:17

January 22

*I have made the
heaven and the earth by
My great power and
outstretched arm, and
there is nothing too hard for Me.*

Jeremiah 32:17

All scripture has been modified for personal edification and encouragement.

January 23

*Call unto Me
and I will
answer thee,
and shew thee
great and
mighty things . . .*

Jeremiah 33:3

January 24

*Believe in Me
that you
will not perish,
but have
eternal life.*

John 3:15

All scripture has been modified for personal edification and encouragement.

January 25

I have chosen you in Me before the foundation of the world, that you should be holy and without blame before Me in love.

Ephesians 1:4

January 26

Because My Son hath made you free, ye shall be free indeed.

John 8:36

All scripture has been modified for personal edification and encouragement.

January 27

And ye shall serve Me, and shall bless thy bread, and thy water, and I will take sickness away from the midst of thee.

Exodus 23:25

January 28

The Spirit of the Lord is upon you.

Luke 4:18

All scripture has been modified for personal edification and encouragement.

January 29

My Word shall not pass away.

Matthew 24:35

January 30

You are strong in spirit, filled with wisdom, and My grace is upon thee.

Luke 2:40

All scripture has been modified for personal edification and encouragement.

January 31

My compassions fail not. They are new every morning: great is My faithfulness.

Lamentations 3:23

February 1

As far as the east is from the west, so far have I removed your transgressions from you.

Psalm 103:12

All scripture has been modified for personal edification and encouragement.

February 2

You are like a tree planted by the rivers of water, that bringest forth fruit in your season; your life shall not wither; and whatsoever you do shall prosper.

Psalm 1:3

February 3

I forgive all thine iniquities and heal all thy diseases.

Psalm 103:3

All scripture has been modified for personal edification and encouragement.

February 4

*I will bless thee and keep thee;
I will make My face
shine upon thee, and
be gracious unto thee.
I will lift up My
countenance upon thee,
and give thee peace.*

Numbers 6:24-26

February 5

*I will deliver you from
your enemies and lift
you up above those
who rise up against
you. I will deliver
you from the violent man.*

Psalm 18:48

All scripture has been modified for personal edification and encouragement.

February 6

I will gird thee with strength, and make your way perfect.

Psalm 18:32

February 7

I have the power to tread down your enemies.

Psalm 108:13

All scripture has been modified for personal edification and encouragement.

February 8

Because I am in you . . . Thou art clothed with honor and majesty.

Psalm 104:1

February 9

I am your strength and your redeemer.

Psalm 19:14

All scripture has been modified for personal edification and encouragement.

FEBRUARY 10

Wherever you go, I am with you . . .

Psalm 23:4

FEBRUARY 11

Be of good courage, and I shall strengthen your heart . . .

Psalm 31:24

All scripture has been modified for personal edification and encouragement.

February 12

*I am your light and your
salvation; do not fear.
I am the strength
of your life;
do not be afraid.*

Psalm 27:1

February 13

*I am your rock
and your fortress;
I will lead you
and guide you.*

Psalm 31:3

All scripture has been modified for personal edification and encouragement.

February 14

*I will instruct thee
and teach thee
in the way which
thou shalt go:
I will guide thee
with Mine eye.*

Psalm 32:8

February 15

*Let your heart
rejoice in Me
as you trust in
My holy name.*

Psalm 33:21

All scripture has been modified for personal edification and encouragement.

February 16

*I am
your help
and
your shield.*

Psalm 33:20

February 17

*As you seek Me,
I hear you,
and will
deliver
you from
all your fears.*

Psalm 34:4

All scripture has been modified for personal edification and encouragement.

February 18

Delight yourself in Me, and I will give you the desires of your heart.

Psalm 37:4

February 19

I am your refuge and strength, a very present help in trouble.

Psalm 46:1

All scripture has been modified for personal edification and encouragement.

February 20

I am the health of your countenance, and your God.

Psalm 43:5

February 21

I will lead you in righteousness because of your enemies; I shall make your way straight before My face.

Psalm 5:8

All scripture has been modified for personal edification and encouragement.

February 22

Cast your burdens upon Me; I shall sustain thee . . .

Psalm 55:22

February 23

My lovingkindness will not be taken from thee, nor will I cause My faithfulness to fail thee.

Psalm 89:33

All scripture has been modified for personal edification and encouragement.

February 24

I am good and ready to forgive; I am filled with mercy when you call upon Me.

Psalm 86:5

February 25

Ye shall call upon Me and I will answer thee. I will be with you in trouble: I will deliver you and honour you.

Psalm 91:15

All scripture has been modified for personal edification and encouragement.

February 26

To him who overcometh will I give to eat of the tree of life . . .

Revelation 2:7

February 27

You have been justified freely by grace through the redemption found in My Son, Jesus Christ.

Romans 3:24

All scripture has been modified for personal edification and encouragement.

February 28

Follow after things which make for peace.

Romans 14:19

February 29

Because I made you free from sin, you have now become a servant of righteousness.

Romans 6:18

All scripture has been modified for personal edification and encouragement.

March 1

I will cause you who love Me to inherit substance; I will fill your treasures.

Proverbs 8:21

March 2

Put your trust in Me and rejoice. Shout for joy because I will defend you.

Psalm 5:11

All scripture has been modified for personal edification and encouragement.

March 3

*You are more than
a conqueror
through Jesus
Who first
loved you.*

Romans 8:37

March 4

*I will show you the path
of life: in My presence
is fulness of joy;
at My right hand are
pleasures for evermore.*

Psalm 16:11

All scripture has been modified for personal edification and encouragement.

March 5

My redeemed shall return to Zion with songs and everlasting joy . . . you shall obtain joy and gladness, sorrow and sighing shall flee away.

Isaiah 35:10

March 6

I will turn your mourning into dancing; I have girded thee with gladness.

Psalm 30:11

All scripture has been modified for personal edification and encouragement.

March 7

I give to men good in My sight: wisdom, knowledge, and joy . . .

Ecclesiastes 2:26

March 8

Don't worry about the days of your life because I will answer you in the joy of your heart!

Ecclesiastes 5:20

All scripture has been modified for personal edification and encouragement.

MARCH 9

My lovingkindness and My truth shall continually preserve thee.

Psalm 40:11

MARCH 10

As you first seek My kingdom and My righteousness, all things shall be added unto you.

Matthew 6:33

All scripture has been modified for personal edification and encouragement.

March 11

*I will redeem your life
from destruction;
I will crown thee
with lovingkindness
and tender mercies.*

Psalm 103:4

March 12

*I have filled you with
My spirit: in wisdom,
and in understanding,
and in knowledge;
in all manner
of workmanship.*

Exodus 31:3

All scripture has been modified for personal edification and encouragement.

March 13

Death and life are in the power of your tongue: so choose life!

Proverbs 18:21

March 14

If ye are of Me, ye will hear My words by My Spirit.

John 8:47

All scripture has been modified for personal edification and encouragement.

March 15

*I am the way,
the truth, and the life;
you cannot come
to Me but
through My Son.*

John 14:6

March 16

*I will
give you
understanding
in all things.*

2 Timothy 2:7

All scripture has been modified for personal edification and encouragement.

March 17

Because you have
set your love
upon Me,
I will
deliver you . . .

Psalm 91:14

March 18

My left hand is under
your head, and
My right hand doth
embrace thee!

Song of Solomon 2:6

All scripture has been modified for personal edification and encouragement.

March 19

You are My beloved, and My desire is toward thee!

Song of Solomon 7:10

March 20

My love is in your heart by the Holy Ghost which has been given unto you.

Romans 5:5

All scripture has been modified for personal edification and encouragement.

March 21

*I will make you
increase and abound
in love one
toward another.*

1 Thessalonians 3:12

March 22

*My mercy is great
above the heavens:
and My truth
reacheth unto
the clouds.*

Psalm 108:4

All scripture has been modified for personal edification and encouragement.

March 23

Nothing shall be able to separate you from My love, which is in Christ Jesus!

Romans 8:39

March 24

I am the Word that will be a lamp unto your feet and a light unto your path.

Psalm 119:105

All scripture has been modified for personal edification and encouragement.

March 25

Hide My Word in your heart . . .

Psalm 119:11

March 26

Praise Me . . . for you are fearfully and wonderfully made . . .

Psalm 139:14

All scripture has been modified for personal edification and encouragement.

March 27

I will perfect that which concerneth you . . .

Psalm 138:8

March 28

I heal your broken heart, and bind up your wounds.

Psalm 147:3

All scripture has been modified for personal edification and encouragement.

March 29

*Your eye cannot see
nor your ear hear
the things that
I have prepared
for you because
you love Me.*

1 Corinthians 2:9

March 30

*I have given you
a spirit of power,
and of love,
and a sound mind.*

2 Timothy 1:7

All scripture has been modified for personal edification and encouragement.

March 31

As you walk
in the Spirit,
you will not
fulfill the lust
of the flesh.

Galatians 5:16

April 1

I am longsuffering,
and of great
mercy, forgiving
your iniquity
and
transgressions . . .

Numbers 14:18

All scripture has been modified for personal edification and encouragement.

April 2

*Give thanks unto
Me for I am good;
My mercy
endureth for ever.*

1 Chronicles 16:34

April 3

*You will have life
and peace when you
choose to be
spiritually minded.*

Romans 8:6

All scripture has been modified for personal edification and encouragement.

April 4

I have delivered you from the power of darkness, and have translated you into the kingdom of My dear Son:

Colossians 1:13

April 5

When you put off the conversation of the old man, I will renew you in the spirit of your mind.

Ephesians 4:22-24

All scripture has been modified for personal edification and encouragement.

April 6

Your new man is renewed in knowledge after the image of My Son.

Colossians 3:10

April 7

As you commit your way unto Me, trust in Me, and I shall bring it to pass.

Psalm 37:5

All scripture has been modified for personal edification and encouragement.

April 8

Your barns shall be filled with plenty and thy presses will burst out with new wine.

Proverbs 3:10

April 9

You are blessed when you hunger and thirst after righteousness: for ye shall be filled.

Matthew 5:6

All scripture has been modified for personal edification and encouragement.

April 10

*For I know the thoughts
that I think toward
you, thoughts of peace,
and not of evil,
to give you
an expected end.*

Jeremiah 29:11

April 11

*My child, give Me
your heart,
and let your
eyes observe
My ways.*

Proverbs 23:26

All scripture has been modified for personal edification and encouragement.

April 12

You shall seek Me, and find Me when you search for Me with all your heart.

Jeremiah 29:13

April 13

Walk in My love, as Christ has loved you, and given Himself for you . . .

Ephesians 5:2

All scripture has been modified for personal edification and encouragement.

April 14

Wait on Me: be of good courage, and I will strengthen your heart.

Psalm 27:14

April 15

I will lift up My countenance upon thee, and give thee peace.

Numbers 6:26

All scripture has been modified for personal edification and encouragement.

April 16

*I am good
unto you when
you wait for Me;
when your soul
seeks after Me.*

Lamentations 3:25

April 17

*Trust in Me,
keep your mind
stayed on Me,
and I will
keep you in
perfect peace.*

Isaiah 26:3

All scripture has been modified for personal edification and encouragement.

April 18

I will make you dwell in safety.

Psalm 4:8

April 19

I have delivered your soul in peace from the battle that was against you.

Psalm 55:18

All scripture has been modified for personal edification and encouragement.

April 20

I will give strength unto you and bless you with peace.

Psalm 29:11

April 21

Let not your heart be troubled, nor let it be afraid. Receive My peace.

John 14:27

All scripture has been modified for personal edification and encouragement.

April 22

*My peace, which passeth
all understanding,
shall keep your heart
and mind through
Christ Jesus.*

Philippians 4:7

April 23

*Ask, and it shall be given you;
seek and ye
shall find; knock,
and it shall be
opened unto you.*

Matthew 7:7

All scripture has been modified for personal edification and encouragement.

April 24

*I will command
My lovingkindness
in the daytime,
and in the night
My song shall
be with thee . . .*

Psalm 42:8

April 25

*And whatsoever
ye shall ask
in My name,
that will I do,
that I may be
glorified in My Son.*

John 14:13

All scripture has been modified for personal edification and encouragement.

April 26

As you wait on Me, integrity and uprightness will preserve thee.

Psalm 25:21

April 27

I create new heavens and a new earth; the former shall not be remembered, nor come into mind.

Isaiah 65:17

All scripture has been modified for personal edification and encouragement.

April 28

*I am your hiding place;
I will preserve thee
from trouble; I will
compass thee about
with songs
of deliverance.
Selah.*

Psalm 32:7

April 29

*And I will restore to
you the years that the
locust hath eaten,
the cankerworm,
and the caterpillar,
and the palmerworm . . .*

Joel 2:25

All scripture has been modified for personal edification and encouragement.

April 30

*Bring ye all the tithes
into the storehouse,
that there may be meat
in your house . . .
see if I will not open
you the windows of heaven,
and pour you out a blessing . . .*

Malachi 3:10

May 1

*Ye were sealed
with that holy
Spirit
of promise.*

Ephesians 1:13

All scripture has been modified for personal edification and encouragement.

May 2

I will abide with you for ever.

John 14:16

May 3

Blessed is the man who endureth temptation: for when you are tried, you shall receive the crown of life . . .

James 1:12

All scripture has been modified for personal edification and encouragement.

May 4

Behold, I will do a new thing in you . . . I will make a way in the wilderness and rivers in the desert.

Isaiah 43:19

May 5

I have given you eternal life in My Son.

1 John 5:11

All scripture has been modified for personal edification and encouragement.

May 6

*All things in your life
work together for good
when you love Me.
You have been called
with a purpose.*

Romans 8:28

May 7

*If you obey and serve
Me, you shall
spend your days
in prosperity,
and your years
in pleasures.*

Job 36:11

All scripture has been modified for personal edification and encouragement.

May 8

Let the Lord be magnified, Who hath pleasure in your prosperity as My servant.

Psalm 35:27

May 9

I have an inheritance incorruptible and undefiled, that does not fade away, reserved in heaven for you.

1 Peter 1:4

All scripture has been modified for personal edification and encouragement.

May 10

*I am your God;
I am your shield,
and the horn of your
salvation, your high tower,
and your refuge, your saviour;
I save thee from violence.*

2 Samuel 22:3

May 11

*I am your Lord,
and a shield for thee;
your glory and
the lifter up
of your head.*

Psalm 3:3

All scripture has been modified for personal edification and encouragement.

May 12

I will bless the righteous; with favour; I will compass you as with a shield.

Psalm 5:12

May 13

I shall cover thee with My feathers, and under My wings shalt thou trust: My truth shall be thy shield and buckler.

Psalm 91:4

All scripture has been modified for personal edification and encouragement.

May 14

*As your heart trusts in Me,
I am your strength
and shield; and you
are helped: therefore
your heart
greatly rejoices . . .*

Psalm 28:7

May 15

*When thou passest
through the waters,
I will be with thee;
and through the rivers,
they shall not
overflow thee.*

Isaiah 43:2a

All scripture has been modified for personal edification and encouragement.

May 16

When thou walkest through the fire, thou shalt not be burned; neither shall the flame kindle upon thee.

Isaiah 43:2b

May 17

I, the Lord, will be a refuge for the oppressed, a refuge in times of trouble.

Psalm 9:9

All scripture has been modified for personal edification and encouragement.

May 18

No weapon that is formed
against thee shall prosper;
and every tongue
that shall rise against
thee in judgment
I will condemn.

Isaiah 54:17

May 19

I shall give
my angels
charge over thee,
to keep thee:

Luke 4:10

All scripture has been modified for personal edification and encouragement.

May 20

I shall guide thee continually, and satisfy thy soul in drought, and make fat thy bones: and thou shalt be like a watered garden, and like a spring of water, whose waters fail not.

Isaiah 58:11

May 21

I am able to keep you from falling, and to present you faultless before the presence of My glory with exceeding joy.

Jude 1:24

All scripture has been modified for personal edification and encouragement.

May 22

I shall supply all your needs according to My riches in glory by Christ Jesus.

Philippians 4:19

May 23

I gave myself for you, that I might redeem you from all iniquity . . .

Titus 2:14

All scripture has been modified for personal edification and encouragement.

May 24

Draw nigh to Me and I will draw nigh to you . . .

James 4:8

May 25

When you dwell in the secret place of the most High ye shall abide under the shadow of the Almighty.

Psalm 91:1

All scripture has been modified for personal edification and encouragement.

May 26

If you confess your sins, I am faithful and just to forgive you your sins, and to cleanse you from all unrighteousness.

1 John 1:9

May 27

Ye are washed, but ye are sanctified, but ye are justified in the name of the Lord Jesus, and by My Spirit.

1 Corinthians 6:11

All scripture has been modified for personal edification and encouragement.

May 28

I have saved you, and called you with an holy calling, not according to your works, but according to My own purpose and grace . . .

2 Timothy 1:9

May 29

I satisfy your mouth with good things so that you youth is renewed like the eagle's.

Psalm 103:5

All scripture has been modified for personal edification and encouragement.

May 30

You have redemption through the blood of Jesus and the forgiveness of sins according to the riches of My grace.

Ephesians 1:7

May 31

You will be transformed by the renewing of your mind, through My Word.

Romans 12:2

All scripture has been modified for personal edification and encouragement.

June 1

Though your outward man perish, your inward man is renewed day by day.

2 Corinthians 4:16

June 2

Come unto Me . . . and I will give you rest.

Matthew 11:28

All scripture has been modified for personal edification and encouragement.

June 3

*I am mighty in your midst;
I will save you and rejoice
over you with joy.
I will rest in your love;
I will joy over thee
with singing.*

Zephaniah 3:17

June 4

*I will
uphold
the righteous.*

Psalm 37:17b

All scripture has been modified for personal edification and encouragement.

June 5

*I will be your God
who goes with you,
to fight for you
against your enemies,
to save you.*

Deuteronomy 20:4

June 6

*I will restore unto thee the joy
of your salvation;
and uphold thee with
My free spirit.*

Psalm 51:12

All scripture has been modified for personal edification and encouragement.

June 7

But if you shall indeed obey My voice, and do all that I speak, then I will be an enemy unto your enemies . . .

Exodus 23:22

June 8

I will answer thee when you call upon Me in the day of your trouble.

Psalm 86:7

All scripture has been modified for personal edification and encouragement.

June 9

I will preserve you from all evil: I will preserve your soul.

Psalm 121:7

June 10

. . . I am the light of the world: if you follow Me you shall not walk in darkness, but shall have the light of life.

John 8:12

All scripture has been modified for personal edification and encouragement.

June 11

Though you walk in the midst of trouble, I will revive thee: I will stretch forth My hand against the wrath of your enemies and My right hand shall save thee.

Psalm 138:7

June 12

He was crucified for you, and the life which you now live in the flesh you live by the faith of My Son, who loved you and gave Himself for you.

Galatians 2:20

All scripture has been modified for personal edification and encouragement.

June 13

Yet I am the Lord thy God from the land of Egypt, and you shalt know no god but Me for there is no saviour beside Me.

Hosea 13:4

June 14

To the end I will establish your heart unblameable in holiness before Me . . . at the coming of your Lord Jesus Christ with all His saints.

1 Thessalonians 3:13

All scripture has been modified for personal edification and encouragement.

June 15

You are of Me, and I have made you an overcomer because greater is He that is in you, than he that is in the world.

1 John 4:4

June 16

I am the God of peace who will sanctify you wholly . . .

1 Thessalonians 5:23

All scripture has been modified for personal edification and encouragement.

June 17

Christ was once offered to bear the sins of many, and unto them that look for Him shall He appear the second time without sin unto salvation.

Hebrews 9:28

June 18

I am the Lord God who is with thee to help thee.

Isaiah 50:7

All scripture has been modified for personal edification and encouragement.

June 19

*As you regardeth
reproof
you shall
be honoured.*

Proverbs 13:18

June 20

*There is nothing from outside
you, that entering into you
can defile: but the things
which come out of you,
those are they that
will defile you.*

Mark 7:15

All scripture has been modified for personal edification and encouragement.

June 21

I will keep your soul, and deliver you. When you put your trust in Me you will not be ashamed.

P salm 25:20

June 22

I am faithful to stablish you and keep you from evil.

2 Thessalonians 3:3

All scripture has been modified for personal edification and encouragement.

June 23

*I am your God
and I shall
deliver you out
of the hand
of all your enemies.*

2 Kings 17:39

June 24

*As you
persevere,
I will
deliver you.*

2 Timothy 3:11

All scripture has been modified for personal edification and encouragement.

June 25

For I so loved the world that
I gave My only begotten
Son, that if you will
believe in Him you
will not perish,
but have everlasting life.

John 3:16

June 26

But if thou shalt seek Me,
thou shalt find Me, if thou
seekest Me with all
thy heart and with
all thy soul.

Deuteronomy 4:29

All scripture has been modified for personal edification and encouragement.

June 27

*I am able to make all grace abound
toward you; that ye, always
having all sufficiency
in all things, may abound
to every good work:*

2 Corinthians 9:8

June 28

*If you sow
in tears
ye shall
reap in joy.*

Psalm 126:5

All scripture has been modified for personal edification and encouragement.

June 29

*. . . I the Lord God
will cause righteousness
and praise to
spring forth before
all the nations.*

Isaiah 61:11

June 30

*For if ye sow to your flesh
ye shall reap
corruption, but if
ye sow to the Spirit
ye shall reap
life everlasting.*

Galatians 6:8

All scripture has been modified for personal edification and encouragement.

July 1

*Be not deceived;
I am not mocked:
for whatsoever
you sow, that shall
ye also reap . . .*

Galatians 6:7

July 2

*I will give beauty for ashes, the
oil of joy for mourning, the
garment of praise for the
spirit of heaviness;
that ye might be called
a tree of righteousness . . .*

Isaiah 61:3

All scripture has been modified for personal edification and encouragement.

July 3

*That the righteousness
of the law might be fulfilled
in you, as you walk
not after the flesh,
but after the Spirit.*

Romans 8:4

July 4

*But if ye be led
of the Spirit,
ye are not
under the law.*

Galatians 5:18

All scripture has been modified for personal edification and encouragement.

July 5

For if you are led by My Spirit, then you are a son of God.

Romans 8:14

July 6

The Spirit of God has made thee, and the breath of the Almighty has given thee life.

Job 33:4

All scripture has been modified for personal edification and encouragement.

July 7

*I will teach you
to do My will,
for I am
your God . . .
I will lead you
into the land of uprightness.*

Psalm 143:10

July 8

*Be strong and of a good courage,
fear not, nor be afraid;
for I do go with
thee; I will not fail
thee nor forsake thee.*

Deuteronomy 31:6

All scripture has been modified for personal edification and encouragement.

July 9

*Do ye not know that
ye are My temple,
and that My Spirit
dwelleth in you?*

1 Corinthians 3:16

July 10

*Your flesh and heart faileth:
but I am the strength
of your heart,
and your portion
for ever.*

Psalm 73:26

All scripture has been modified for personal edification and encouragement.

July 11

Wait upon Me and I shall renew your strength; ye shall mount up with wings as eagles; ye shall run, and not be weary; and shall walk, and not faint.

Isaiah 40:31

July 12

You can do all things through Christ because I strengthen you.

Philippians 4:13

All scripture has been modified for personal edification and encouragement.

July 13

*Glory in your
infirmities,
that the power
of My Son
may rest upon you.*

2 Corinthians 12:9b

July 14

*. . . I am faithful;
I will not suffer you to
be tempted above that
ye are able; but will
make a way of escape . . .*

1 Corinthians 10:13

All scripture has been modified for personal edification and encouragement.

July 15

Submit yourself to Me. Resist the devil, and he will flee from you.

James 4:7

July 16

Praise My name with a song and magnify Me with thanksgiving.

Psalm 69:30

All scripture has been modified for personal edification and encouragement.

July 17

Watch and pray, that ye enter not into temptation: your spirit indeed is willing, but your flesh is weak.

Matthew 26:41

July 18

Enter into My gates with thanksgiving, and into My courts with praise: be thankful to Me and bless My name.

Psalm 100:4

All scripture has been modified for personal edification and encouragement.

July 19

And let the peace of God rule in your heart, to the which also are ye called in one body; and be ye thankful.

Colossians 3:15

July 20

But thanks be to Me, who gives you the victory through your Lord Jesus Christ.

1 Corinthians 15:57

All scripture has been modified for personal edification and encouragement.

July 21

*It is a good thing to
give thanks unto Me,
and to sing praises
unto My name . . .*

Psalm 92:1

July 22

*But lay up for yourself treasures in
heaven, where neither moth
or rust can corrupt,
where thieves do not
break through nor steal . . .*

Matthew 6:20

All scripture has been modified for personal edification and encouragement.

July 23

With treasures of darkness and hidden riches of secret places, you will know that I am the Lord which call thee by name that I am the God of Israel.

Isaiah 45:3

July 24

Honour Me with thy substance, and with the firstfruits of all thine increase.

Proverbs 3:9

All scripture has been modified for personal edification and encouragement.

July 25

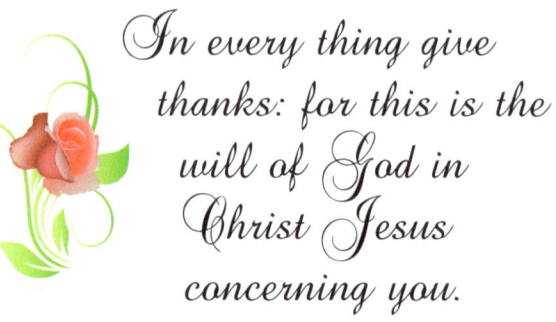

In every thing give thanks: for this is the will of God in Christ Jesus concerning you.

1 Thessalonians 5:18

July 26

For where your treasure is, there will your heart be also.

Matthew 6:21

All scripture has been modified for personal edification and encouragement.

July 27

In Me are hid all the treasures of wisdom and knowledge.

Colossians 2:3

July 28

In the world ye shall have tribulation: but be of good cheer; I have overcome the world.

John 16:33b

All scripture has been modified for personal edification and encouragement.

July 29

*. . . If thou turn to Me
and shall be obedient
unto My voice,
I will not forsake thee,
neither destroy thee . . .*

Deuteronomy 4:30

July 30

*Nothing shall separate you from
the love of Christ. Not
tribulation, nor distress,
nor persecution, nor
famine, nor nakedness,
nor peril, nor sword.*

Romans 8:35

All scripture has been modified for personal edification and encouragement.

July 31

*I comfort you in all
your tribulation,
that you may be able
to comfort them
which are in trouble.*

2 Corinthians 1:4

August 1

*It is better to
trust in Me
than to
put confidence
in man.*

Psalm 118:8

All scripture has been modified for personal edification and encouragement.

August 2

O taste and see that I am good: blessed are you who trusteth in Me.

Psalm 34:8

August 3

Trust in Me with all your heart; and lean not unto your own understanding. In all thy ways acknowledge Me, and I shall direct your paths.

Proverbs 3:3-6

All scripture has been modified for personal edification and encouragement.

August 4

Every word of Mine is pure: I am a shield unto you when you put your trust in Me.

Proverbs 30:5

August 5

I will teach you My ways; you will walk in My truth: I will unite your heart to fear My name.

Psalm 86:11

All scripture has been modified for personal edification and encouragement.

August 6

*Behold, I desire truth
in your inward parts:
and in the hidden part
I will make you
to know wisdom.*

Psalm 51:6

August 7

*For I am good;
My mercy is everlasting;
and My truth
endureth to
all generations.*

Psalm 100:5

All scripture has been modified for personal edification and encouragement.

August 8

*Now is the time
when true worshippers
shall worship Me
in spirit
and in truth . . .*

John 4:23

August 9

*Ye know My spirit of truth;
for I dwell
with you,
and shall be
in you.*

John 14:17

All scripture has been modified for personal edification and encouragement.

August 10

And ye shall
know the truth,
and the truth
shall make
you free!

John 8:32

August 11

When the Spirit of truth is come,
He will guide you into all
truth . . . that whatsoever
He shall hear, that He
will speak; and He will
show you things to come.

John 16:13

All scripture has been modified for personal edification and encouragement.

August 12

*For you can do
nothing against
the truth,
but for the truth.*

2 Corinthians 13:8

August 13

*Behold, how good and how
pleasant it is for
My children
to dwell
together in unity!*

Psalm 133:1

All scripture has been modified for personal edification and encouragement.

August 14

Serve Me with gladness: come before My presence with singing.

Psalm 100:2

August 15

Let My Word dwell in you richly in all wisdom; teaching and admonishing one another in psalms and hymns and spiritual songs . . .

Colossians 3:16

All scripture has been modified for personal edification and encouragement.

August 16

*Through Me
ye shall do valiantly:
for it is I
who shall tread down
your enemies.*

Psalm 60:12

August 17

*You shall not die,
but live,
and declare
the works
of Mine.*

Psalm 118:17

All scripture has been modified for personal edification and encouragement.

August 18

*For I am
your defence;
and the Holy
One of Israel
is your king.*

Psalm 89:18

August 19

*O sing unto Me a new song;
for I have done marvellous
things: My right hand,
and My holy arm, hath
gotten you the victory.*

Psalm 98:1

All scripture has been modified for personal edification and encouragement.

August 20

*I will swallow up
death in victory;
and I will
wipe away tears
from off your face . . .*

Isaiah 25:8

August 21

*. . . Ye are strong,
and My word
abideth in you,
and ye have overcome
the wicked one.*

1 John 2:14b

All scripture has been modified for personal edification and encouragement.

August 22

*. . . You shall arise;
when you sit
in darkness,
I shall be
a light unto thee.*

Micah 7:8

August 23

*For whatsoever is born of Me
overcometh the world:
and this is the victory
that overcometh the world,
even your faith.*

1 John 5:4

All scripture has been modified for personal edification and encouragement.

August 24

And you overcome him by the blood of the Lamb, and by the word of your testimony.

Revelation 12:11

August 25

Hearken now unto My voice, I will give thee counsel, and I shall be with thee . . .

Exodus 18:19

All scripture has been modified for personal edification and encouragement.

August 26

. . . If there be any virtue, and if there be any praise, think on these things.

Philippians 4:8

August 27

Blessed are you . . . I am your strength, who teachs your hands to war, and your fingers to fight:

Psalm 144:1

All scripture has been modified for personal edification and encouragement.

August 28

*. . . They that war
against thee shall
be as nothing,
and as a thing
of nought.*

Isaiah 41:12

August 29

*Commit your
works unto Me,
and your thoughts
shall be established.*

Proverbs 16:3

All scripture has been modified for personal edification and encouragement.

August 30

*For though
ye walk
in the flesh,
ye need not war
after the flesh . . .*

2 Corinthians 10:3

August 31

*If ye are willing
and obedient,
ye shall eat
the good
of the land.*

Isaiah 1:19

All scripture has been modified for personal edification and encouragement.

September 1

*If you live
in the Spirit,
be sure to walk
in the Spirit.*

Galatians 5:25

September 2

*Discretion shall
preserve thee,
understanding
shall keep thee.*

Proverbs 2:11

All scripture has been modified for personal edification and encouragement.

September 3

*I give wisdom:
out of My mouth
comes knowledge
and understanding.*

Proverbs 2:6

September 4

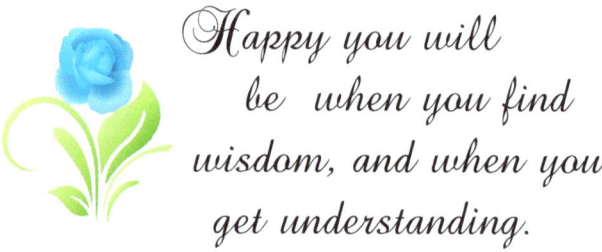

*Happy you will
be when you find
wisdom, and when you
get understanding.*

Proverbs 3:13

All scripture has been modified for personal edification and encouragement.

September 5

*When you lie down,
you shall not
be afraid . . .
and your sleep
shall be sweet.*

Proverbs 3:24

September 6

*The heart of the wise teacheth
your mouth,
and addeth
learning
to your lips.*

Proverbs 16:23

All scripture has been modified for personal edification and encouragement.

September 7

When you handle a matter wisely you shall find good: and you will be happy when you trust in Me.

Proverbs 16:20

September 8

You wrestle not against flesh and blood, but against principalities, powers, and the rulers of the darkness of this world, against spiritual wickedness in high places.

Ephesians 6:12

All scripture has been modified for personal edification and encouragement.

September 9

*But when ye
walk wisely,
ye shall
be delivered.*

Proverbs 28:26b

September 10

*When you bless yourself
in the earth, you
shall bless yourself
in Me, the God
of truth . . .*

Isaiah 65:16

All scripture has been modified for personal edification and encouragement.

SEPTEMBER 11

Be not rash with your mouth, and let not thine heart be hasty to utter any thing before Me: for I am in heaven . . . therefore let thy words be few.

Ecclesiastes 5:2

SEPTEMBER 12

For I satisfy your longing soul, and fill your hungry soul with goodness.

Psalm 107:9

All scripture has been modified for personal edification and encouragement.

September 13

If you lack wisdom, ask Me, who gives to all men liberally, and upbraids not.

James 1:5

September 14

Be swift to hear, slow to speak, and slow to wrath.

James 1:19

All scripture has been modified for personal edification and encouragement.

September 15

But My wisdom that is from above is first pure, then peaceable, gentle, and easy to be intreated, full of mercy and good fruits, without partiality, and without hypocrisy.

James 3:17

September 16

For in your time of trouble I will hide thee in the secret place; I will set thee up upon a rock.

Psalm 27:5

All scripture has been modified for personal edification and encouragement.

September 17

Fear not: for I have redeemed thee, I have called thee by thy name; thou art Mine.

Isaiah 43:1b

September 18

Therefore I say unto you, What things soever ye desire, when ye pray, believe that ye receive them, and ye shall have them.

Mark 11:24

All scripture has been modified for personal edification and encouragement.

September 19

Jesus said, I am the bread of life: if you come to Me ye shall never hunger; and if you believe on Me, ye shall never thirst.

John 6:35

September 20

I am come a light into the world, that if ye believe on Me ye should not abide in darkness.

John 12:46

All scripture has been modified for personal edification and encouragement.

September 21

*I will
love thee,
and
bless thee,
and multiply thee . . .*

Deuteronomy 7:13

September 22

*. . . But I have called you friend;
for all things that
I have heard
of My Father
I have made
known unto you.*

John 15:15

All scripture has been modified for personal edification and encouragement.

SEPTEMBER 23

If you believe on Me, the works that I do ye shall do also, and greater works than these shall ye do, because I go unto My Father.

John 14:12

SEPTEMBER 24

Humble yourself therefore under My mighty hand, that I may exalt you in due time.

1 Peter 5:6

All scripture has been modified for personal edification and encouragement.

September 25

Study to yourself approved unto Me, a workman that need not be ashamed, rightly dividing the word of truth.

2 Timothy 2:15

September 26

I shall cover you all the day long, and you will dwell between My shoulders.

Deuteronomy 33:12

All scripture has been modified for personal edification and encouragement.

September 27

And He saith unto you, "Follow Me, and I will make you a fisher of men."

Matthew 4:19

September 28

. . . Be perfect, be of good comfort, be of one mind, live in peace; and I, the God of love and peace, shall be with you.

2 Corinthians 13:11

All scripture has been modified for personal edification and encouragement.

SEPTEMBER 29

With men it is impossible, but not with Me: for with Me all things are possible.

Mark 10:27

SEPTEMBER 30

. . . I will hear when you call unto Me.

Psalm 4:3

All scripture has been modified for personal edification and encouragement.

October 1

When thou prayest, enter into thy closet, and when thou hast shut thy door, pray to Me in secret; and I who seeth in secret will reward thee openly.

Matthew 6:6

October 2

Trust in Me at all times; pour out your heart before Me: I am a refuge for you.

Psalm 62:8

All scripture has been modified for personal edification and encouragement.

October 3

When your ways please Me, I will make even your enemies to be at peace with you.

Proverbs 16:7

October 4

I restore your soul: I will lead you in the paths of righteousness for My name's sake.

Psalm 23:3

All scripture has been modified for personal edification and encouragement.

October 5

Since the beginning of the world, you have not perceived by the ear, neither hath your eye seen, what I have prepared for you when you wait upon Me.

Isaiah 64:4

October 6

I will preserve thy going out and thy coming in from this time forth, and even for evermore.

Psalm 121:8

All scripture has been modified for personal edification and encouragement.

October 7

For I the Lord God am a sun and shield: I will give grace and glory: no good thing will I withhold from you for walking uprightly.

Psalm 84:11

October 8

My goodness endureth continually.

Psalm 52:1

All scripture has been modified for personal edification and encouragement.

October 9

Behold, I am your salvation; you will trust, and not be afraid: for I Jehovah am your strength and your song; I am become your salvation.

Isaiah 12:2

October 10

. . . I the Lord shall be your everlasting light, and the days of your mourning shall be ended.

Isaiah 60:20

All scripture has been modified for personal edification and encouragement.

October 11

For ye shall go out with joy, and be led forth with peace . . . and all the trees of the field shall clap their hands.

Isaiah 55:12

October 12

Be still and know that I am God: I will be exalted among you, I will be exalted in the earth.

Psalm 46:10

All scripture has been modified for personal edification and encouragement.

October 13

. . . But My kindness shall not depart from thee, neither shall the covenant of My peace be removed; I have mercy on thee.

Isaiah 54:10

October 14

Surely goodness and mercy shall follow you all the days of your life: you will dwell in the house of the Lord for ever.

Psalm 23:6

All scripture has been modified for personal edification and encouragement.

October 15

*Confess your faults
one to another,
and pray one
for another,
that ye may
be healed.*

James 5:16a

October 16

*When Christ,
who is your life,
shall appear,
then shall you appear
with Him in glory.*

Colossians 3:4

All scripture has been modified for personal edification and encouragement.

October 17

But without faith it is impossible to please Me: for when you come to Me you must believe that I am, and that I am a rewarder as you diligently seek Me.

Hebrews 11:6

October 18

Truly your soul must wait upon Me: from Him cometh your salvation.

Psalm 62:1

All scripture has been modified for personal edification and encouragement.

October 19

I make the storm a calm, so that the waves thereof are still.

Psalm 107:29

October 20

In all thy ways acknowledge Me, and I shall direct your paths.

Proverbs 3:6

All scripture has been modified for personal edification and encouragement.

October 21

My presence shall go with thee, and I will give thee rest.

Exodus 33:14

October 22

Rather seek ye My kingdom; and all these things shall be added unto you.

Luke 12:31

All scripture has been modified for personal edification and encouragement.

October 23

O give thanks unto Me; for I am good: because My mercy endureth for ever.

Psalm 118:1

October 24

For I the Lord thy God will hold your right hand, saying unto you, Fear not; I will help thee.

Isaiah 41:13

All scripture has been modified for personal edification and encouragement.

October 25

I will give you a heart to know Me, that I am your Lord: and you shall be My child, and I will be your God . . .

Jeremiah 24:7

October 26

And they shall fight against thee; but they shall not prevail against thee; for I am with thee . . . to deliver thee.

Jeremiah 1:19

All scripture has been modified for personal edification and encouragement.

October 27

Sing of My power, sing aloud of My mercy in the morning: for I have been your defence and refuge in the day of trouble.

Psalm 59:16

October 28

I am nigh unto you when you call upon Me, when you call upon Me in truth.

Psalm 145:18

All scripture has been modified for personal edification and encouragement.

October 29

*I will uphold
you when you fall,
and raise you up when
you are bowed down.*

Psalm 145:14

October 30

*I have commanded thee to be strong
and of a good courage;
to be not afraid,
nor be dismayed:
for I am with thee
whithersoever thou goest...*

Joshua 1:9

All scripture has been modified for personal edification and encouragement.

October 31

*Behold,
I am your helper:
I am with you
to uphold your soul.*

Psalm 54:4

November 1

*I make you to lie down
in green pastures:
I lead you
beside the
still waters.*

Psalm 23:2

All scripture has been modified for personal edification and encouragement.

November 2

*So that you may
boldly say that
I am your helper,
and you will not fear
what man shall
do unto thee.*

Hebrews 13:6

November 3

*. . . for I am
your defence,
and the God
of your mercy.*

Psalm 59:17

All scripture has been modified for personal edification and encouragement.

November 4

I make your feet like hinds' feet and set you upon My high places.

Psalm 18:33

November 5

I have enlarged your steps under ye, that your feet will not slip.

Psalm 18:36

All scripture has been modified for personal edification and encouragement.

November 6

I have given thee the shield of your salvation: and My right hand hath holden you up, and My gentleness hath made you great.

Psalm 18:35

November 7

I will not suffer your foot to be moved: I keep thee and do not slumber.

Psalm 121:3

All scripture has been modified for personal edification and encouragement.

November 8

*I am your keeper;
I am your shade . . .*

Psalm 121:5

November 9

Having spoiled principalities and powers, I made a show of them openly, triumphantly.

Colossians 2:15

All scripture has been modified for personal edification and encouragement.

November 10

I am faithful. You were called unto the fellowship of My Son Jesus Christ your Lord.

1 Corinthians 1:9

November 11

I am the Lord and good to all: and My tender mercies are over all your works.

Psalm 145:9

All scripture has been modified for personal edification and encouragement.

November 12

*I have made you a
little lower than
the angels,
and have crowned
you with glory and honour.*

Psalm 8:5

November 13

*I will make of thee a great nation,
and I will bless
thee, and make your
name great; and thou
shalt be a blessing.*

Genesis 12:2

All scripture has been modified for personal edification and encouragement.

November 14

By Me you believe and are justified from all things from which ye could not be justified by the law of Moses.

Acts 13:39

November 15

I am merciful and gracious, slow to anger, and plenteous in mercy.

Psalm 103:8

All scripture has been modified for personal edification and encouragement.

November 16

I will not always chide: neither will I keep My anger for ever.

Psalm 103:9

November 17

I have not dealt with you after your sins; nor rewarded you according to your iniquities.

Psalm 103:10

All scripture has been modified for personal edification and encouragement.

November 18

Hear My word and believe on Me who sent Me, so you shall have everlasting life, and shall not come into condemnation, but be passed from death unto life.

John 5:24

November 19

For as the heaven is high above the earth, so great is My mercy toward you when you fear Me.

Psalm 103:11

All scripture has been modified for personal edification and encouragement.

November 20

For I sent not My Son into the world to condemn you, but that you through Him might be saved.

John 3:17

November 21

I am the hope you have as an anchor of your soul, both sure and stedfast . . .

Hebrews 6:19

All scripture has been modified for personal edification and encouragement.

November 22

*If you believe
on Me
you will not
be condemned . . .*

John 3:18

November 23

*Nevertheless you
are continually
with Me:
I hold you
by My right hand.*

Psalm 73:23

All scripture has been modified for personal edification and encouragement.

November 24

*I shall guide you
with My counsel,
and afterward
receive you
to glory.*

Psalm 73:24

November 25

*In My favour is life:
weeping may
endure for a night,
but joy cometh
in the morning.*

Psalm 30:5

All scripture has been modified for personal edification and encouragement.

November 26

Behold, I stand at the door, and knock: if you will hear My voice, and open the door, I will come in to you, and will sup with you, and you with Me.

Revelation 3:20

November 27

I prepare a table before you in the presence of your enemies: I anoint your head with oil; your cup runneth over.

Psalm 23:5

All scripture has been modified for personal edification and encouragement.

November 28

I hold your soul in life, and suffer not your feet to be moved.

Psalm 66:9

November 29

I shall give that which is good; and your land shall yield her increase.

Psalm 85:12

All scripture has been modified for personal edification and encouragement.

November 30

But verily I
have heard thee;
I have attended
to the voice
of your prayer.

Psalm 62:8

December 1

By a new
and living way,
I have consecrated
your flesh, through
the veil . . .

Hebrews 10:20

All scripture has been modified for personal edification and encouragement.

December 2

*I have sealed you,
and given you
the earnest of
the Spirit
in your heart.*

2 Corinthians 1:22

December 3

*For in Me you live,
and move, and have
your being ...
for you are also
My offspring.*

Acts 17:28

All scripture has been modified for personal edification and encouragement.

December 4

How precious also are My thoughts unto thee!

Psalm 139:17a

December 5

For you are unto Me a sweet savour of Christ, both those who are saved, and in those who perish.

2 Corinthians 2:15

All scripture has been modified for personal edification and encouragement.

December 6

*I am the Lord thy God
who teacheth thee
to profit, who leadeth
thee by the way that
thou shouldest go.*

Isaiah 48:17

December 7

*You foresaw Me always
before your face, for I
am on your right hand,
that you should
not be moved.*

Acts 2:25

All scripture has been modified for personal edification and encouragement.

December 8

*For I shall give
My angels
charge over thee,
to keep thee
in all thy ways.*

Psalm 91:11

December 9

*I love you because
you love Me;
and when you
seek Me early
you shall find Me.*

Proverbs 8:17

All scripture has been modified for personal edification and encouragement.

December 10

I have been mindful of you: I will bless you . . .

Psalm 115:12

December 11

Take My yoke upon you, and learn of Me; for I am meek and lowly in heart: and ye shall find rest unto your soul.

Matthew 11:29

All scripture has been modified for personal edification and encouragement.

December 12

I am the God of all grace, who hath called you unto My eternal glory by Christ Jesus . . . make you perfect, stablish, strengthen, settle you.

1 Peter 5:10

December 13

I who search your heart know what is the mind of the Spirit, because He maketh intercession for you according to My will.

Romans 8:27

All scripture has been modified for personal edification and encouragement.

December 14

Likewise My Spirit also helpeth your infirmities: for you know not what you should pray, but My Spirit itself maketh intercession for you . . .

Romans 8:26

December 15

Ye are complete in Me, which is the head of all principality and power.

Colossians 2:10

All scripture has been modified for personal edification and encouragement.

December 16

I will pour water upon you when you are thirsty, and floods upon the dry ground . . .

Isaiah 44:3

December 17

I brought you up also out of an horrible pit, out of the miry clay, and set your feet upon a rock, and established your goings.

Psalm 40:2

All scripture has been modified for personal edification and encouragement.

December 18

I have put a new song in your mouth, even praise unto your God . . .

Psalm 40:3

December 19

For with Me nothing shall be impossible.

Luke 1:37

All scripture has been modified for personal edification and encouragement.

December 20

For My yoke is easy, and My burden is light.

Matthew 11:30

December 21

I will wait and be gracious unto you, that I be exalted, because I have mercy upon you: for I am a God of judgment: blessed are you when you wait for Me.

Isaiah 30:18

All scripture has been modified for personal edification and encouragement.

December 22

That the trial of your faith be tried
with fire, that it might
be found unto praise and
honour and glory
at the appearing
of My Son . . .

1 Peter 1:7

December 23

Not that ye are sufficient
of yourself to think
any thing as of yourself,
but your sufficiency
is of Me.

2 Corinthians 3:5

All scripture has been modified for personal edification and encouragement.

December 24

*For as the sufferings of Christ
abound in you,
so your consolation
also aboundeth
by My Son.*

2 Corinthians 3:5

December 25

*Being a good man,
your steps are ordered
by Me:
and I delighteth
in your way.*

Psalm 37:23

All scripture has been modified for personal edification and encouragement.

December 26

*Though ye fall,
ye shall not be
utterly cast down:
for I upholdeth you
with My hand.*

Psalm 37:24

December 27

*Yea, others
may forget,
yet I
will not
forget thee.*

Isaiah 49:15

All scripture has been modified for personal edification and encouragement.

December 28

A merry heart maketh a cheerful countenance . . .

Proverbs 15:13

December 29

My blessings maketh rich and I addeth no sorrow with it.

Proverbs 10:22

All scripture has been modified for personal edification and encouragement.

December 30

There shall no evil befall thee, neither shall any plague come nigh thy dwelling.

Psalm 91:10

December 31

Beloved, I wish above all things that thou mayest prosper and be in health, even as thy soul prospereth.

3 John 2

All scripture has been modified for personal edification and encouragement.

BOOKS by Kathleen Schubitz

...In His Presence
Intimate moments with your Savior

...In His Presence 40-Day Journal

ABC Journal to Freedom

ABC Woman Finds Freedom

ABCs of Who I Am in Christ!
I Am what God says I Am!

Finding Purpose after Abuse
Exposing enemy lies to empower believers with God's truth

Journal to Freedom

Living With Purpose 30-Day Journal

Lord, I Praise You...

Lord, I Worship You...

Personal Poetic Promises from God's Word

Scripture Keys
Inspiring words for your journey

Many of our books are available in color
as well as black/white.
Some are available in hardcover.

MOST BOOKS ARE AVAILABLE THROUGH AMAZON KINDLE

www.rpjandco1417.com
www.smashwords.com (ebooks in multiple formats)

More Inspiring books by RPJ & Company:

A Symphony of Seasons
by Connie Arnold

Abundant Comfort and Grace
by Connie Arnold

Amazing Grace for Widows
by Jane C. Wittbold

If the Battle is the Lord's... Why Am I So Tired?
by Randy Newberry

**Jesus Invites You...
to the Marriage Supper of the Lamb**
by Jane C. Wittbold

Order in the House!
by Virginia G. Mendes

Peaceful Moments of Love and Light
by Connie Arnold

You Are Loved
by Patricia Elston

MOST BOOKS ARE AVAILABLE THROUGH AMAZON KINDLE

Find more books at most online bookstores:

Amazon.com

and

www.rpjandco1417.com

www.smashwords.com (ebooks in multiple formats)

About the Author

KATHLEEN SCHUBITZ is an accomplished author, poet, speaker and business woman. God's spoken word from Romans 14:17 birthed RPJ & Company (Righteousness, Peace and Joy) in 2004, thereby establishing a Kingdom publishing business for God's people. As founder and president, her faith in God and desire to follow His leading compels her to pursue her own writing and publish books, devotionals, poetry, calendars and marketing materials for leaders and Kingdom writers.

After growing up in the Midwestern United States, Kathleen presently resides in central Florida. Preparation for her calling comes from serving at Rotary International headquarters as production assistant for *The Rotarian* magazine. Having now become an inspirational writer, she lives a life of dedication to God, choosing to turn life's hardships into stepping stones for success. Pressing through an oppressive childhood, life-threatening abuse and sickness as an adult, Kathleen allows the Spirit of God to turn her tragedies into triumph and devastation into dedication. Victorious over her own hurtful situations, she now helps others discover truth to live a life of freedom.

A few of Kathleen's published works include the following: *...In His Presence, Scripture Keys, His Heart Calls, Personal Poetic Promises from God's Word* and *ABCs of Who I Am in Christ!* Her prolific skills in writing, proof-editing, design and typography help new and experienced authors publish books and quality products with a spirit of excellence. To learn more about Kathleen Schubitz or publishing and related services by RPJ & Company, visit: www.rpjandco1417.com.

www.ingramcontent.com/pod-product-compliance
Lightning Source LLC
Chambersburg PA
CBHW041625220426
43663CB00001B/9